This book belongs to:

_____

ABC's
of Healthcare Careers

© 2024

Farihah Amatullah, Hanlin Li, Demetra Tsapepas
All rights reserved.

No part of this book may be reproduced or used in any manner without written permission of the copyright owner except for the use of quotations in a book review.

ABC's

There are many types of healthcare workers. Help your child understand what some of these positions are in this fun book!

Hi there!

My Name is Rx, some people find it easier to call me Rex. I am a prescription, meaning a set of instructions from the doctor to a pharmacist who will provide medicines to a patient to feel better!

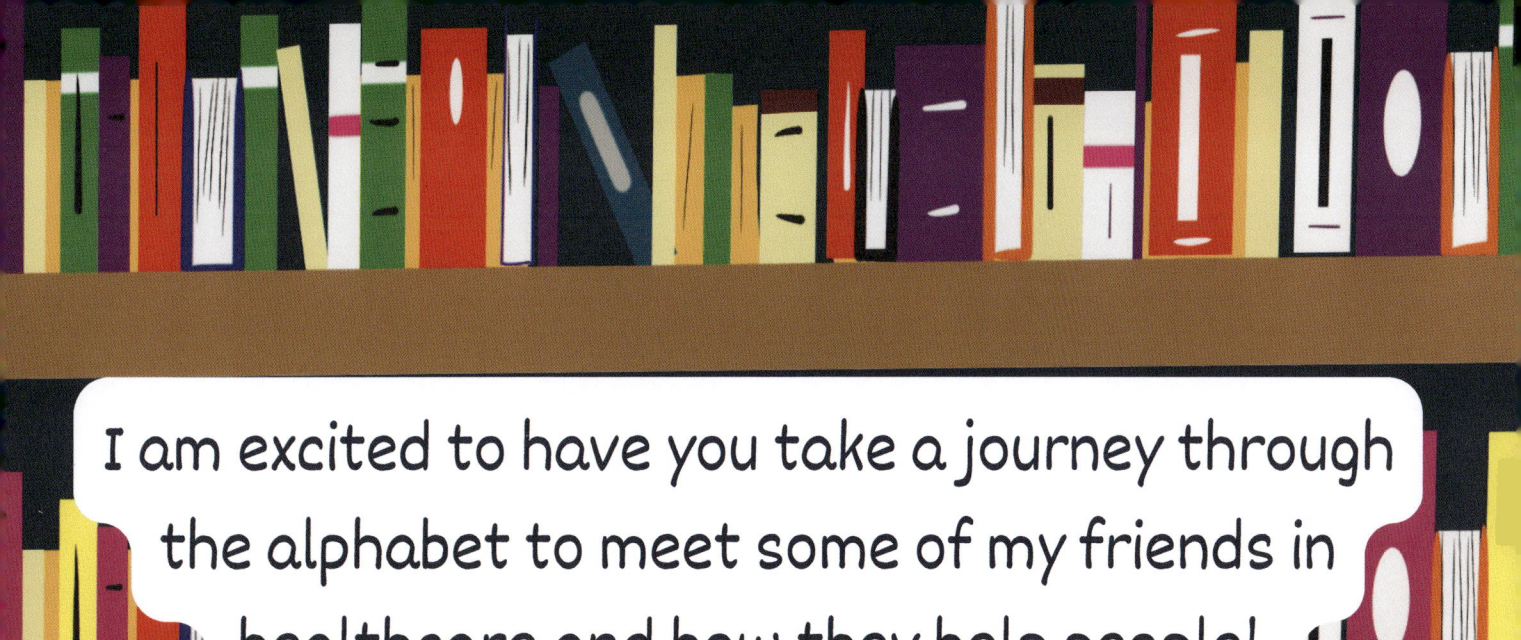

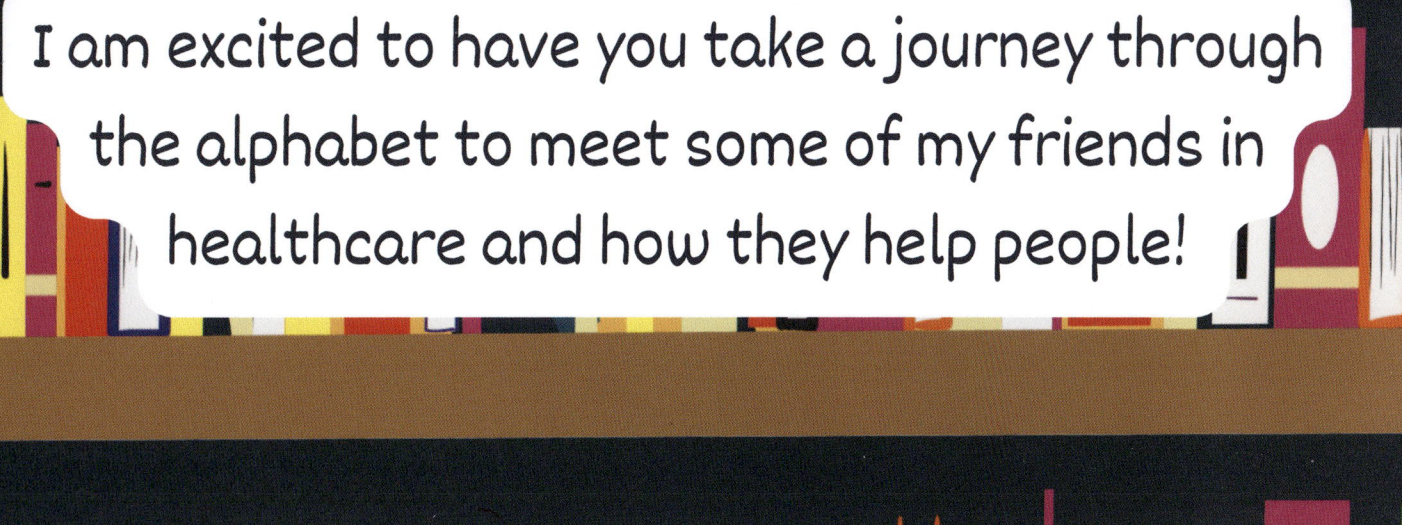

I am excited to have you take a journey through the alphabet to meet some of my friends in healthcare and how they help people!

A IS FOR AUDIOLOGIST

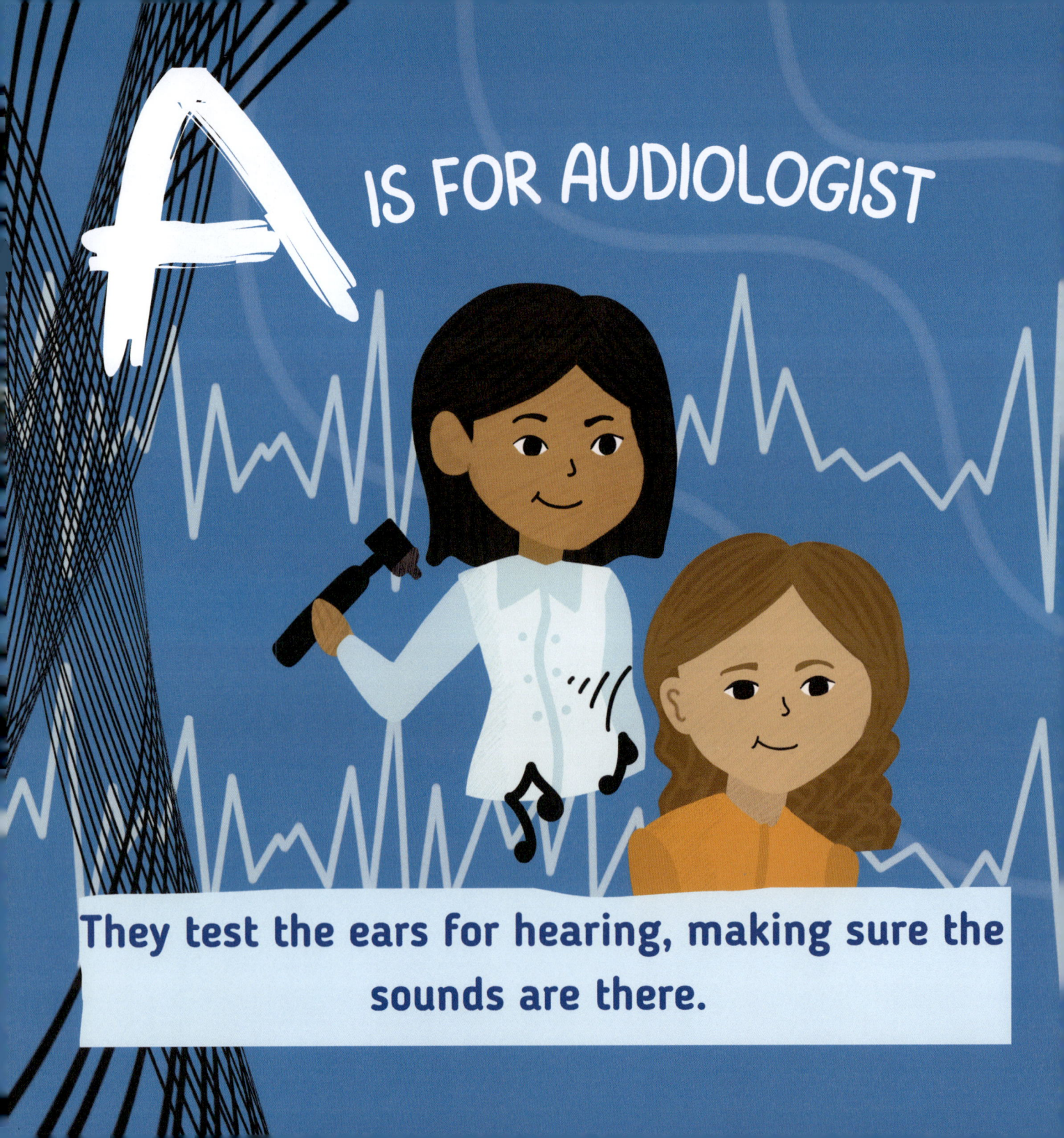

They test the ears for hearing, making sure the sounds are there.

B IS FOR BIOLOGIST

They study living organisms

that are lurking everywhere.

C IS FOR CARDIOLOGIST

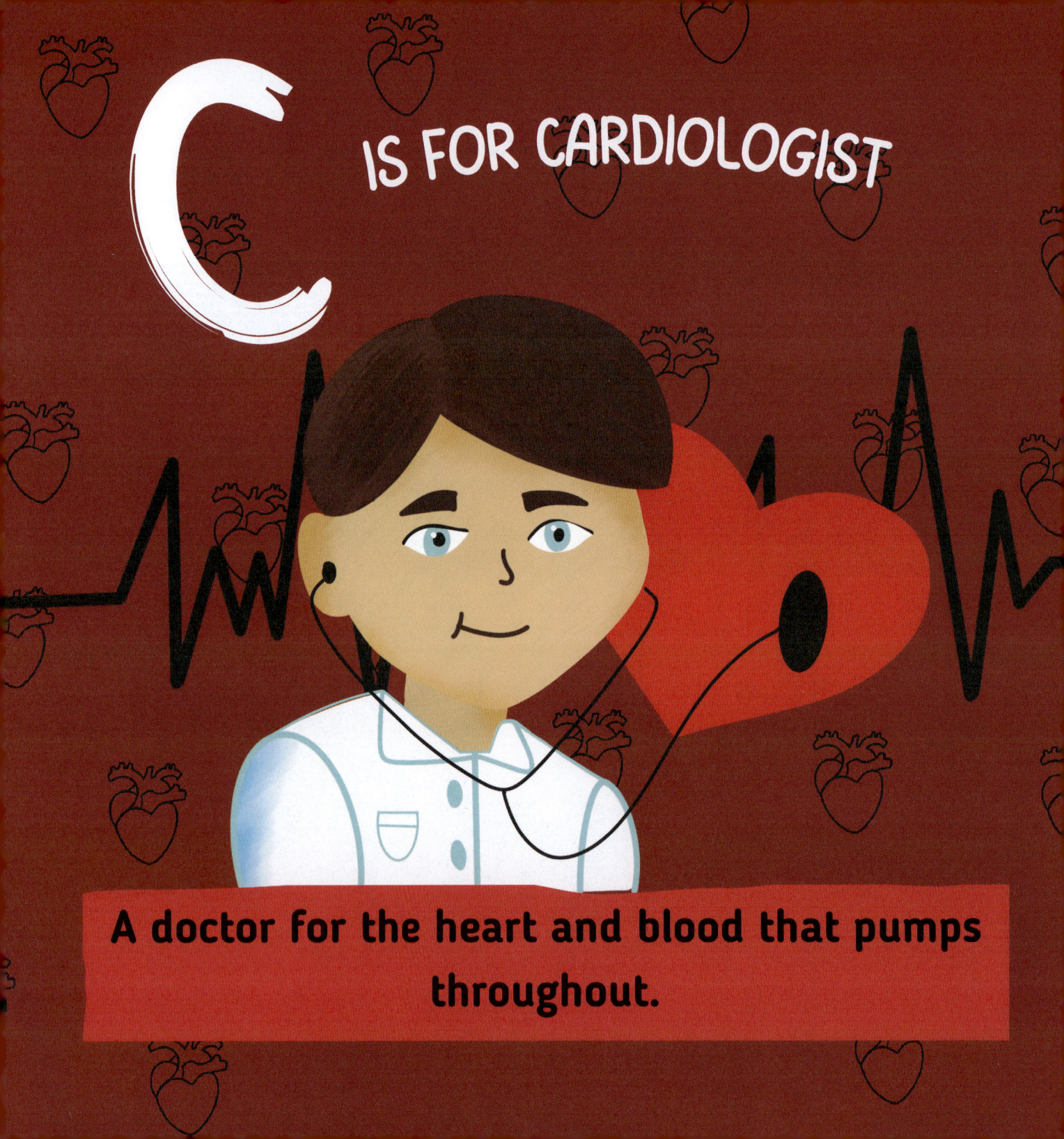

A doctor for the heart and blood that pumps throughout.

D IS FOR DENTIST

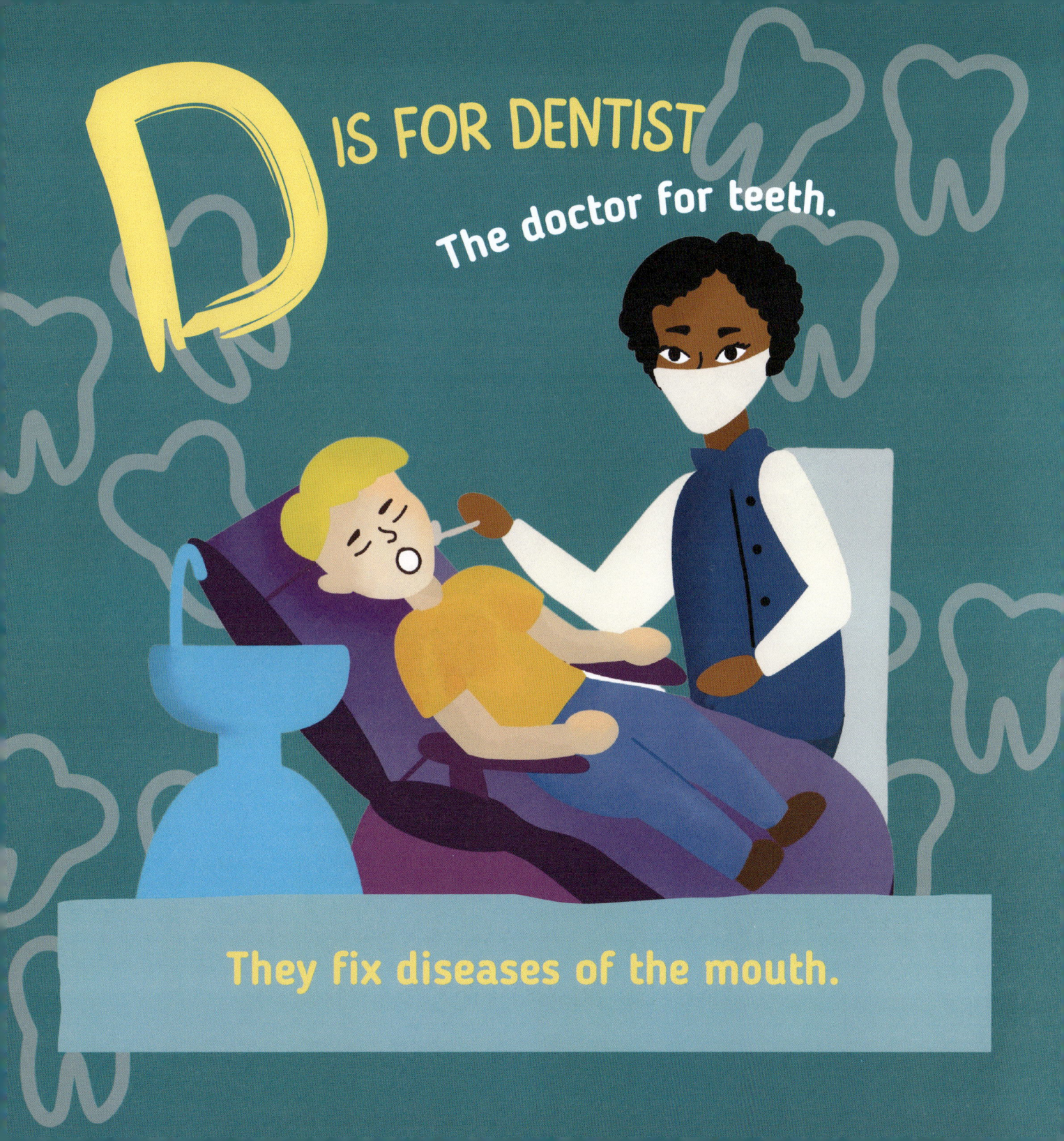

The doctor for teeth.

They fix diseases of the mouth.

E IS FOR EXERCISE PHYSIOLOGIST

They make a fitness program, helping patients to feel strong.

F IS FOR FINANCIAL COORDINATOR

They keep track of all the bills to help treatments move along.

G IS FOR GASTROENTEROLOGIST

They treat the entire digestive system, like the stomach and the mouth.

H IS FOR HEALTHCARE ADMINISTRATOR

They manage offices or hospitals, keeping them organized throughout.

I IS FOR INFORMATICS SPECIALIST

They specialize in technology,

$E=mc^2$

protecting patients behind the scenes.

J IS FOR JOINT COMMISSION SURVEYOR

They inspect hospital sites, making sure the care is clean.

K IS FOR KINESIOLOGIST

They focus on the body's movement so that patients can be healed.

L IS FOR LAB TECHNICIAN

They collect samples from patients and support providers in the field.

M is for Medical Assistant

They take blood pressure, weight, and height, preparing all for care.

N IS FOR NURSE

They support all patients in more ways than one, essential everywhere.

O IS FOR OPTOMETRIST

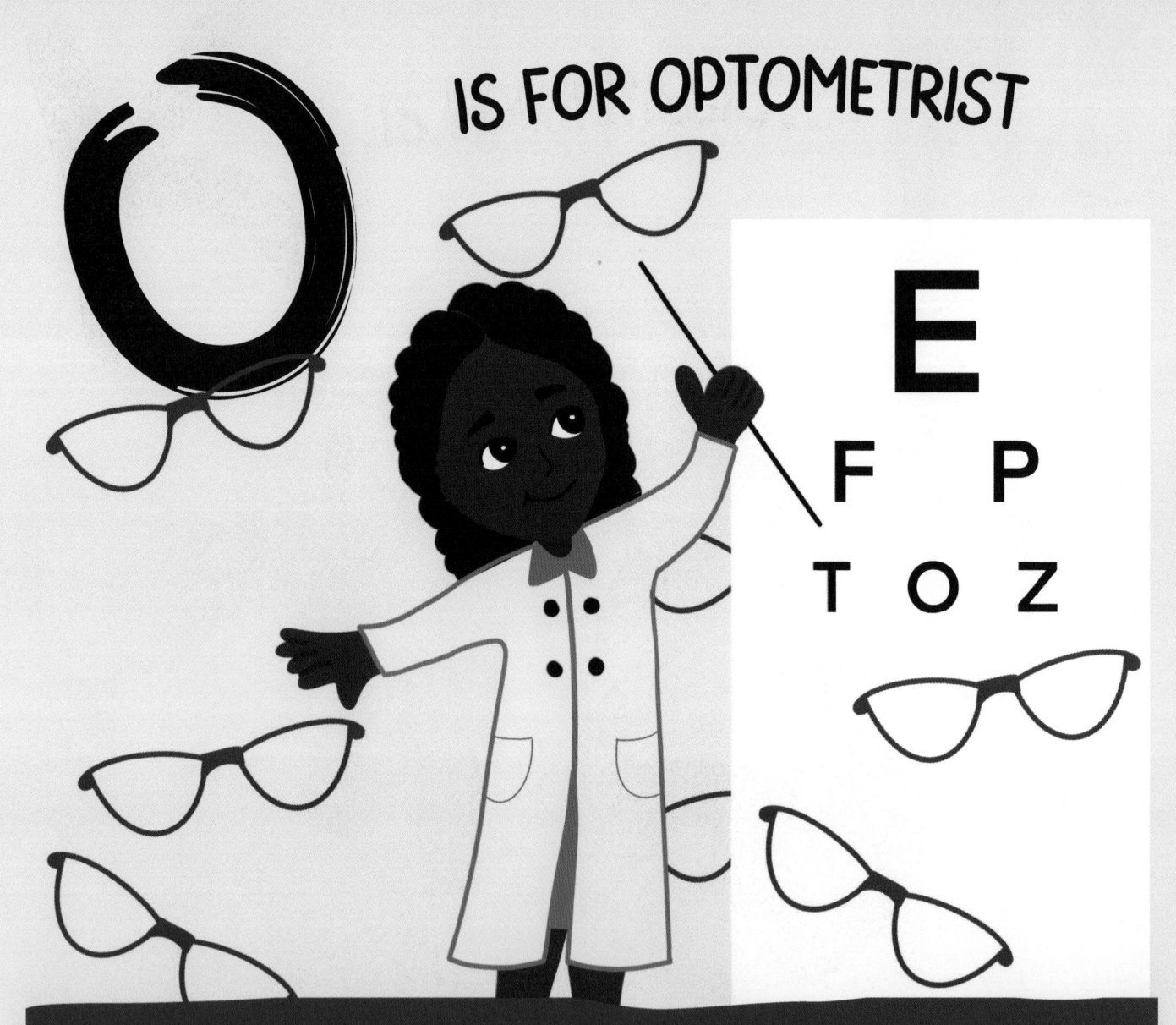

They treat the eyes for vision and health, with tests to check eyesight.

P IS FOR PHARMACIST

They are experts in medications.

They make sure the treatments are right.

Q IS FOR QUALITY OFFICER

They make sure care received is safe and set standards that are high.

R IS FOR RADIOLOGIST

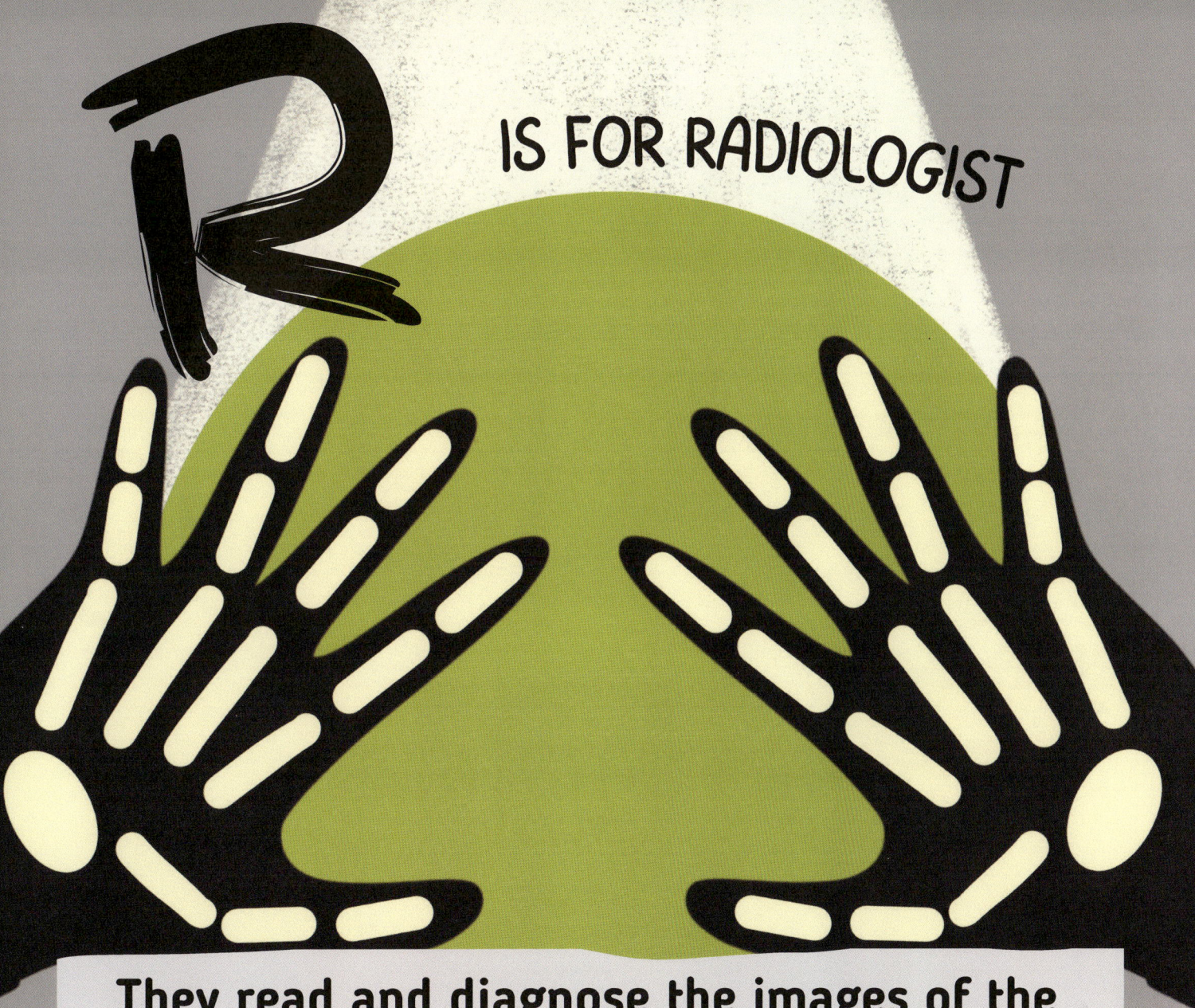

They read and diagnose the images of the body, from X-rays to MRIs.

S IS FOR SURGEON

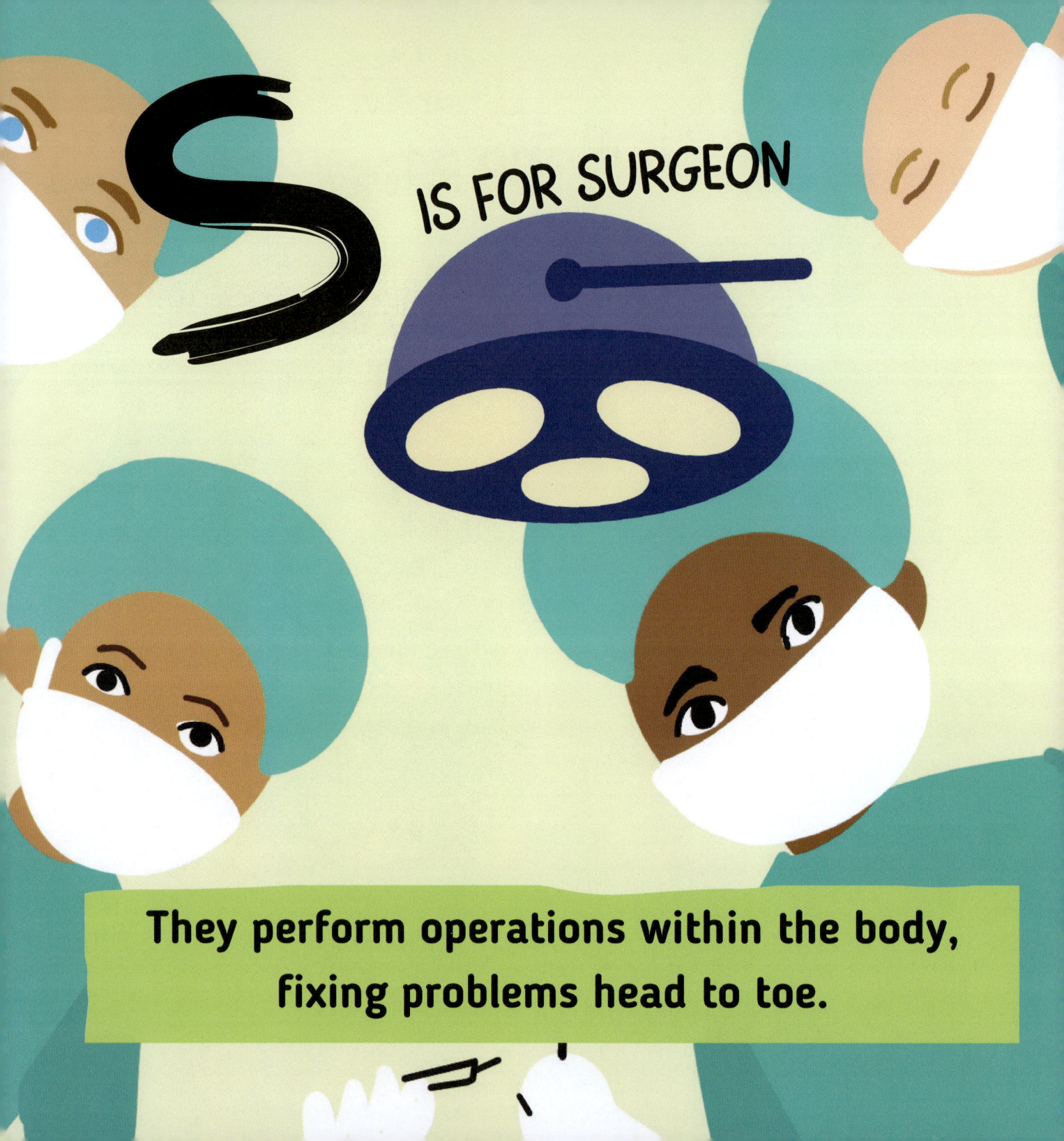

They perform operations within the body, fixing problems head to toe.

T IS FOR THERAPIST

They guide patients through thoughts and feelings from today or long ago.

U IS FOR ULTRASOUND TECHNOLOGIST

They use machines to watch the baby inside the mommy's womb.

V IS FOR VETERINARIAN

They care for pets, whether in the home or roaming in the zoo.

W IS FOR WELLNESS COORDINATOR

They design a program for lifestyle changes for mental health and growth.

X IS FOR X-RAY TECHNICIAN

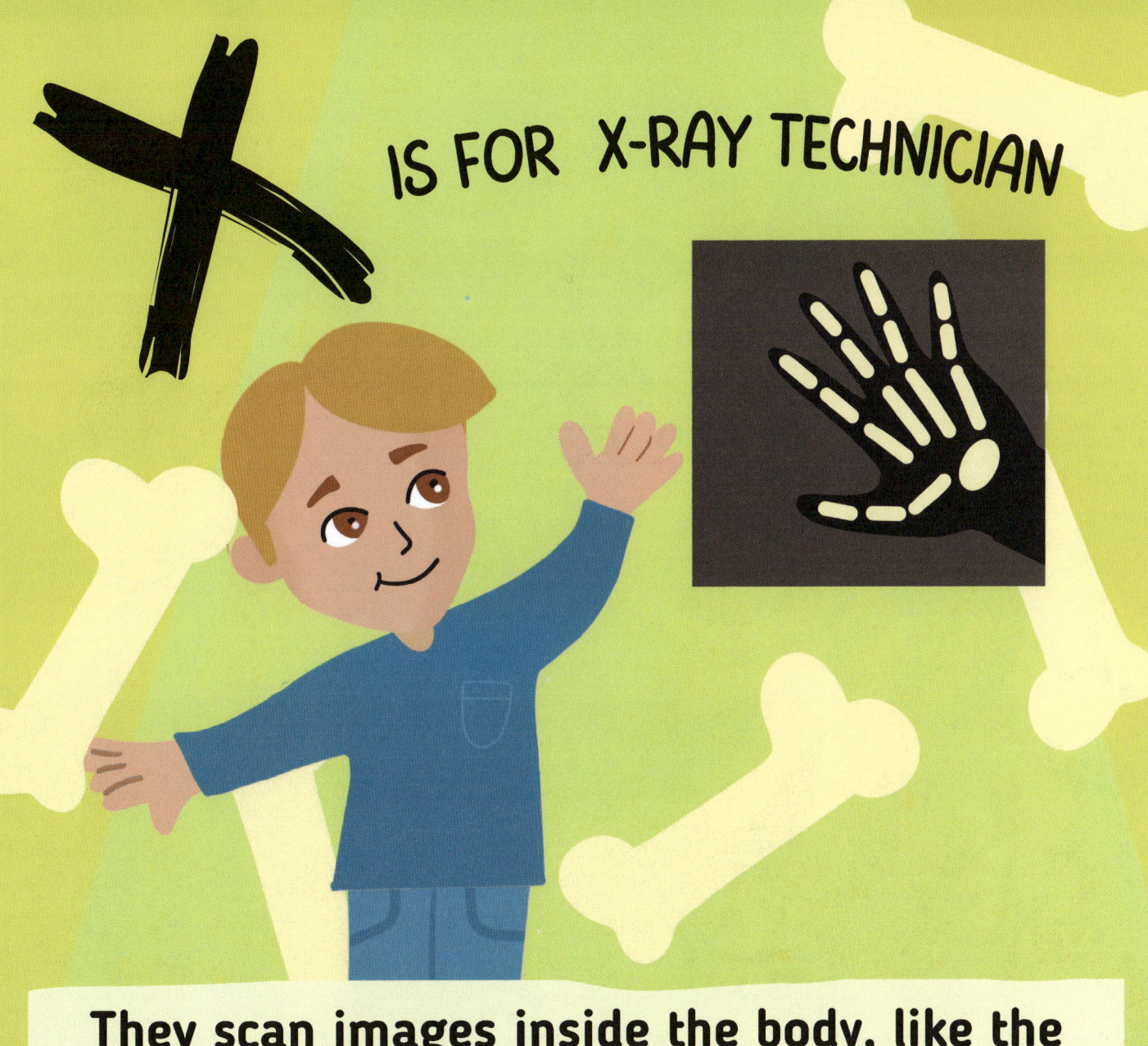

They scan images inside the body, like the bones from head to toe.

Y IS FOR YOUTH COUNSELOR

Your future

They speak to young people about their goals to create a future that is bright.

Z IS FOR ZOOLOGIST

They study and care for animals, in the zoo or out of sight.

Author Team

Dr. Amatullah is a pharmacist, informaticist, and artist. She knows the ins and outs of specialty pharmacy during the day and shifts to taking care of her toddler son and newborn daughter. Her life does not have a dull moment, and now she is even more complete being an author.

Dr. Li is a practicing clinician specializing in chronic disease management with administrative responsibilities and conducting clinical research. She is inspired by her toddler daughter every day and cannot wait to have an influence on the next generation of young scientists.

Dr. Tsapepas is a pharmacist with years of clinical experience who now focuses on quality, education and healthcare research. She is the best Thea Deda to her nephews and nieces who keep her entertained. She would like to extend learning excitement to all.

The three close friends have partnered on multiple projects over the years. Their latest adventure is to create fun educational materials and foster critical thinking in children.

Daskalos Lab

DASKALOS_LAB

Printed in Great Britain
by Amazon